LUDWIG VAN BEETHOVEN

Bagatelles, Rondos and Other Shorter Works for Piano

DOVER PUBLICATIONS, INC., NEW YORK

Published in Canada by General Publishing Company, Ltd., 30 Lesmill Road, Don Mills, Toronto, Ontario.

Published in the United Kingdom by Constable and Company, Ltd., 10 Orange Street, London WC2H 7EG.

This Dover edition, first published in 1987, is a republication of "Serie 18. Kleinere Stücke für das Pianoforte" from *Ludwig van Beethoven's Werke. Vollständige kritisch durchgesehene überall berechtigte Ausgabe. Mit Genehmigung aller Originalverleger*, as originally published by Breitkopf & Härtel, Leipzig (complete set, 1862–1865).

The publisher gratefully acknowledges the cooperation of the Paul Klapper Library, Queens College, New York City, for the loan of material reprinted in this volume.

Manufactured in the United States of America
Dover Publications, Inc., 31 East 2nd Street, Mineola, N.Y. 11501

Library of Congress Cataloging-in-Publication Data

Beethoven, Ludwig van, 1770–1827.
[Piano music. Selections]
Bagatelles, rondos and other shorter works for piano.

Reprint. Originally published: Leipzig : Breitkopf & Härtel, 1862–1865. Originally published in series: Ludwig van Beethoven's Werke.
1. Piano music. I. Title.
M22.B4D66   1987   86-755453
ISBN 0-486-25392-9

CONTENTS

SEVEN BAGATELLES
Op. 33

Andante grazioso, quasi allegretto.

N.° 1.

SCHERZO.
Allegro.

N.º 2.

Minore.

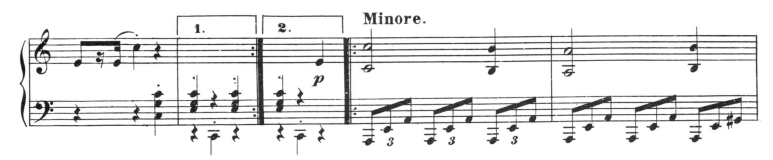

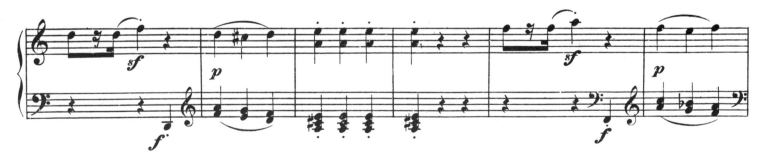

Trio.

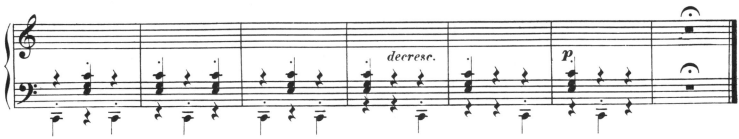

Allegretto.

N̲o̲ 3.

Andante.

Nº 4.

Allegro ma non troppo.

No. 5.

Allegretto quasi andante.

Con una certa espressione parlante.

No. 6.

Presto.

N.º 7.

TWO PRELUDES THROUGH ALL TWELVE MAJOR KEYS
Op. 39

Nº 1.

calando - - - pp

Nº 2.

RONDO, C MAJOR
Op. 51/1

Moderato e grazioso.

RONDO, G MAJOR
Op. 51/2

Andante cantabile e grazioso.

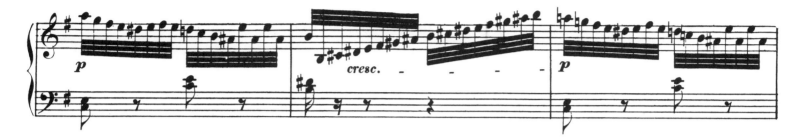

Allegretto.

Tempo I.

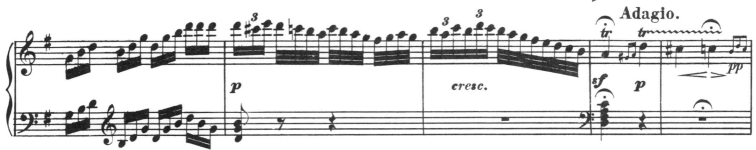

FANTASIA
G MINOR/B-FLAT MAJOR
Op. 77

Allegro ma non troppo.

Adagio.

Allegretto.

POLONAISE, C MAJOR
Op. 89

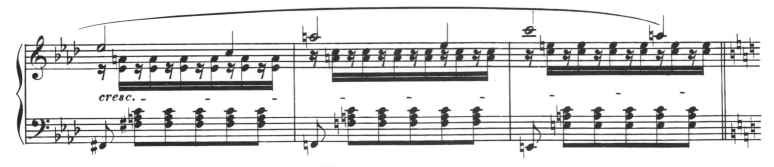

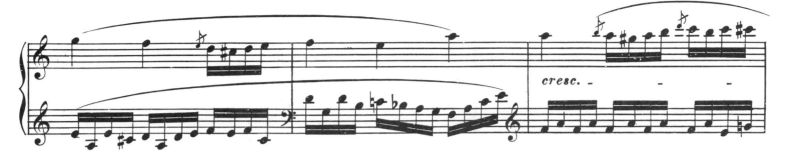

Ossia:

Poco adagio.

Il tempo primo.

ELEVEN BAGATELLES
Op. 119

Allegretto.

Nº 1.

Andante con moto.

Nº 2.

à l'Allemande

Nº 3.

Ped.　❈　Ped.　❈

Ped.　❈　Ped.　❈

Coda.

Da capo fin al segno 𝄌
ed allora la Coda.

Andante cantabile.

N.º 4.

N⁰ 5.

Risoluto.

N⁰ 6.

Andante.

Allegretto. Leichtlich vorgetragen.

leggiermente

molto leggiermente

a tempo

un poco ritard. - - -

L'istesso tempo. (Dieselbe Bewegung.)

stringendo il tempo

N.o 7.

SIX BAGATELLES
Op. 126

Andante con moto.
Cantabile e compiacevole.

Nº 1.

L'istesso tempo.

molto ten.

non troppo presto.

La seconda parte due volte.

Allegro.

Nº 2.

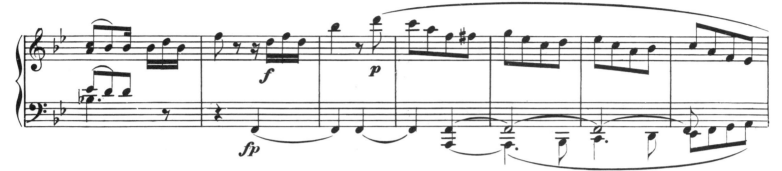

Cantabile.

Andante.
Cantabile e grazioso.

№ 3.

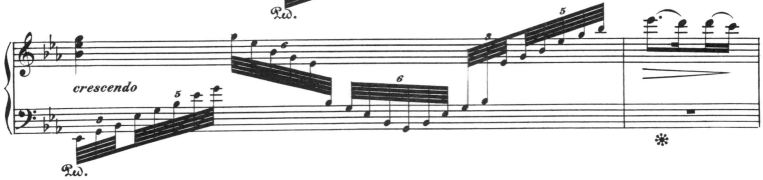

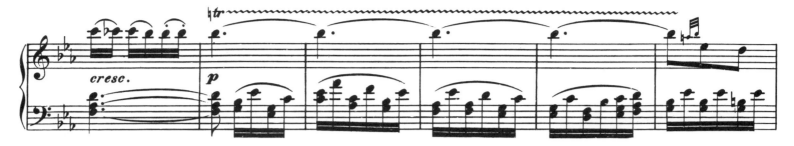

Presto.

No 4.

Quasi allegretto.

N⁰ 5.

Presto.

No. 6.

Andante amabile e con moto.

RONDO A CAPRICCIO
G MAJOR, Op. 129
("Rage over a Lost Penny")

ANDANTE
F MAJOR, WoO 57
("Andante favori")

Andante grazioso con moto.

MINUET, E-FLAT MAJOR
WoO 82

Moderato.

Trio.

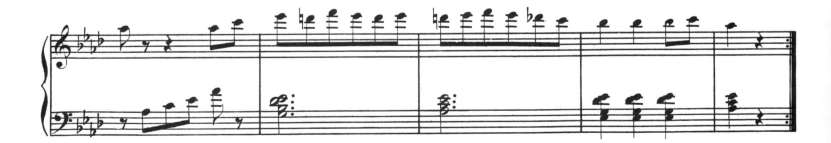

Menuetto da capo.

SIX MINUETS
WoO 10

Nº 1.

Men. da capo.

Nº 2.

Trio.

Men. da capo.

N⁰ 3.

Trio.

Men. da capo.

Nᵒ 4.

Trio.

Men. da capo.

№ 5.

Trio.

Men. da capo.

N⁰ 6.

Trio.

Men. da capo.

PRELUDE, F MINOR
WoO 55

RONDO, A MAJOR
WoO 49

SIX LÄNDLER

Nº 1.

Nº 2.

N.º 3.

N.º 4.

N.º 5.

Nº 6.

CODA.

SEVEN LÄNDLER
WoO 11

Nº 1.

Nº 2.

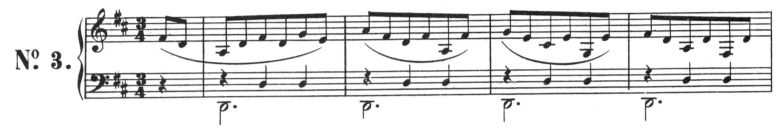

N.º 3.

N.º 4.

Nº 5.

Nº 6.

N° 7.

Coda.